SoCAL So Cool

TRAVEL BOOK

_____

YOUR NAME HERE

The publisher has made every effort to ensure that the contents of this book was current at the time of publication. It is always best to confirm information before making final travel plans as information is always subject to change. The publisher cannot accept responsibility for any consequences arising from the use of this book. Assessment of attractions and so forth are based upon the authors' own experiences; therefore, descriptions given in this book necessarily contain an element of subjective opinion.

SoCal So Cool: Travel Book is an independent publication and has not been reviewed by the following entities and is in no way authorized, endorsed or approved by the companies, its sponsors, partners or affiliates:
Six Flags of America, Ronald Reagan Presidential Library, Malibu Riders, Paramount Ranch, The Getty Center, City of Beverly Hills, La Brea Tar Pit, Los Angeles County Museum Arts, Hollywood Walk of Fame, Hollywood Chamber of Commerce, Hollywood Bowl, Universal Studios Hollywood, Griffith Observatory, Rose Parade, Los Angeles Dodgers, Staples Center, Los Angeles Lakers, Los Angeles Clippers, Los Angeles Kings, Los Angeles Sparks, City of Santa Monica, Pacific Park Amusement Park on the Santa Monica Pier, City of Venice Beach, City of Big Bear Lake, Knott's Berry Farm, Disneyland Anaheim, Disney California Adventure, City of Newport Beach, Balboa Pier, Santa Catalina Island, Legoland California, Los Angeles County Fair, Ventura County Fair, Orange County Fair, San Diego Zoo, San Diego Safari Park, SeaWorld San Diego

Please send comments and suggestions via the below website.

RectorTales.com

Text copyright © Ryan Ashley Rector & Clarence Rector

Illustrations by Oscar Herrero
Illustrations copyright © Clarence Rector

Narrative Panels Design by Clarence Rector
Credits to FreePik

Front Cover Design by Clarence Rector
Front Cover Illustration by Cesar Medina

Back Cover Design by Clarence Rector
Credits to Freepik

ISBN/SKU: 9780996908559
ISBN Complete: 978-0-9969085-5-9

Library of Congress Control Number: 2016945816

Printed in the United States of America

First Printing, 2017

Acknowledgments

Special thanks to our illustrator, Oscar Herrero, for his great work, flexibility, and patience.

Thanks again to our moms (Kali Rector & Helen Dewey) for their full support.

Thanks to Walt Disney, Walter Knott, and other visionaries who created all of the magical places that make SoCal one of the best places to live and visit.

Welcome to SoCal So Cool Travel Book!

This is a one of a kind book that will show you all of the COOL places to go and COOL things to do in SoCal. By the way, SoCal is a shortened way to say Southern California. Long ago, California was sort of split up into two sides, Northern and Southern, because they didn't get along. Today, they all get along, but people continue to use Southern California to describe the lower region of the state. SoCal is mostly made up of the major cities Los Angeles and San Diego, but it also includes many other amazing cities such as Valencia, Burbank, Pasadena, Big Bear Lake, Beverly Hills, Anaheim, Santa Barbara, Newport Beach and many others.

Okay enough of the history lesson! Let's get back to the COOL stuff. This book was written to show that SoCal is one of the coolest places in the world for kids. Why? Well to start off, it has seven theme parks! Many places only have one. It also has many fun beaches and even has a couple of islands. Then there's Hollywood which is a magical place on its own. Let me just show you why So Cal is So COOL.

Enjoy,
Ryan

APOCALYPSE
The Ride
If you're really brave, take a leap off the Dive Devil.
Full Throttle features the worlds tallest vertical loop!
SUPERMAN
Scape from Krypton
Ride the New Revolution while wearing a virtual reality headset. You will feel like you're in another world.
Bugs Bunny World created just for younger kids.
SIX FLAGS
MAGIC MOUNTAIN
X2

Get ready to scream as you drop on Superman!

Ride one of the world's most famous coasters, Twisted Colossus.

TWISTED COLOSSUS

Six Flags Magic Mountain, also known as the Thrill Capital of the World, is located in my hometown, Valencia, California. It opened in 1971 as Magic Mountain with 33 attractions, featuring the Gold Rusher and an observation tower called Sky Tower. In 1978, Colossus roller coaster became the fastest dual track wooden coaster on earth. Currently, Six Flags Magic Mountain has the most roller coasters in the world. So, if you love roller coasters, then Six Flags Magic Mountain is the place to be!

Interesting Fact: Magic Mountain was actually created with the help of SeaWorld in a partnership with Newhall Land and Farming Company.

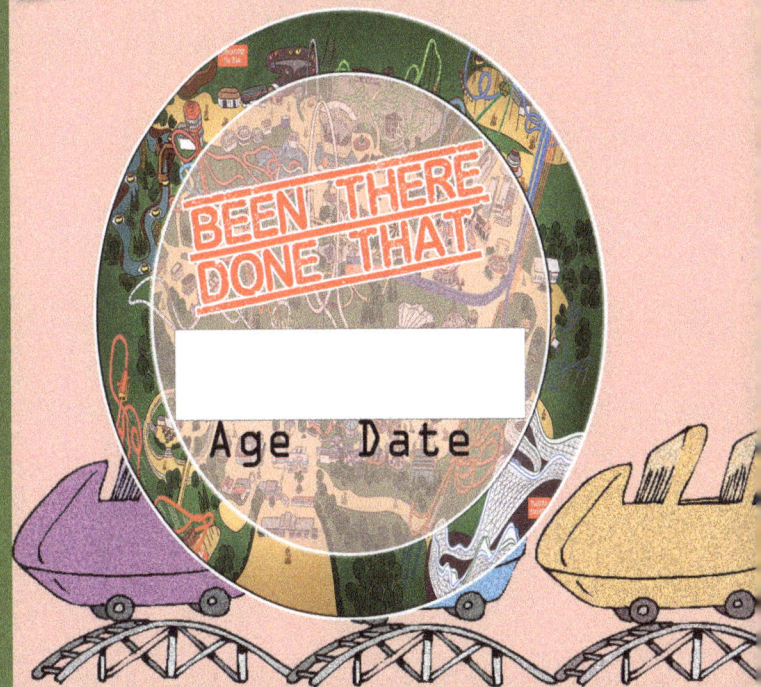

BEEN THERE DONE THAT

Age   Date

Get a close up look at President Reagan's office.

Ronald Reagan Presidential Library, located in Simi Valley, opened in November, 1981. It is a museum for the resting place of the United States' 40th President. Most of the exhibits have something to do with Ronald Reagan's life, but the museum also features special exhibits such as "Interactive! The Exhibit" (a hands on experience with latest and future tech stuff like virtual reality goggles, robots, games and so much more), "Christmas Around the World" (26 Christmas Trees from around the world), "Baseball: The Exhibition", and many more cool exhibits.

Fun Fact: How did they get that huge airplane inside the library?
The plane was actually taken apart piece by piece at the San Bernardino International Airport and then driven to the library. After all of the parts were delivered, the plane was put back together inside the library.

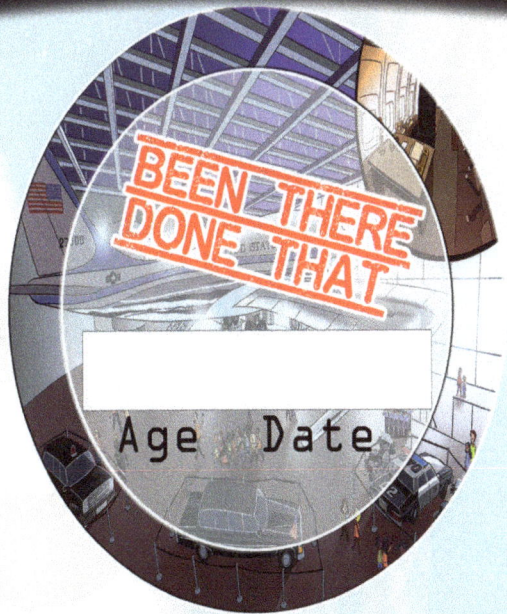

BEEN THERE DONE THAT

Age   Date

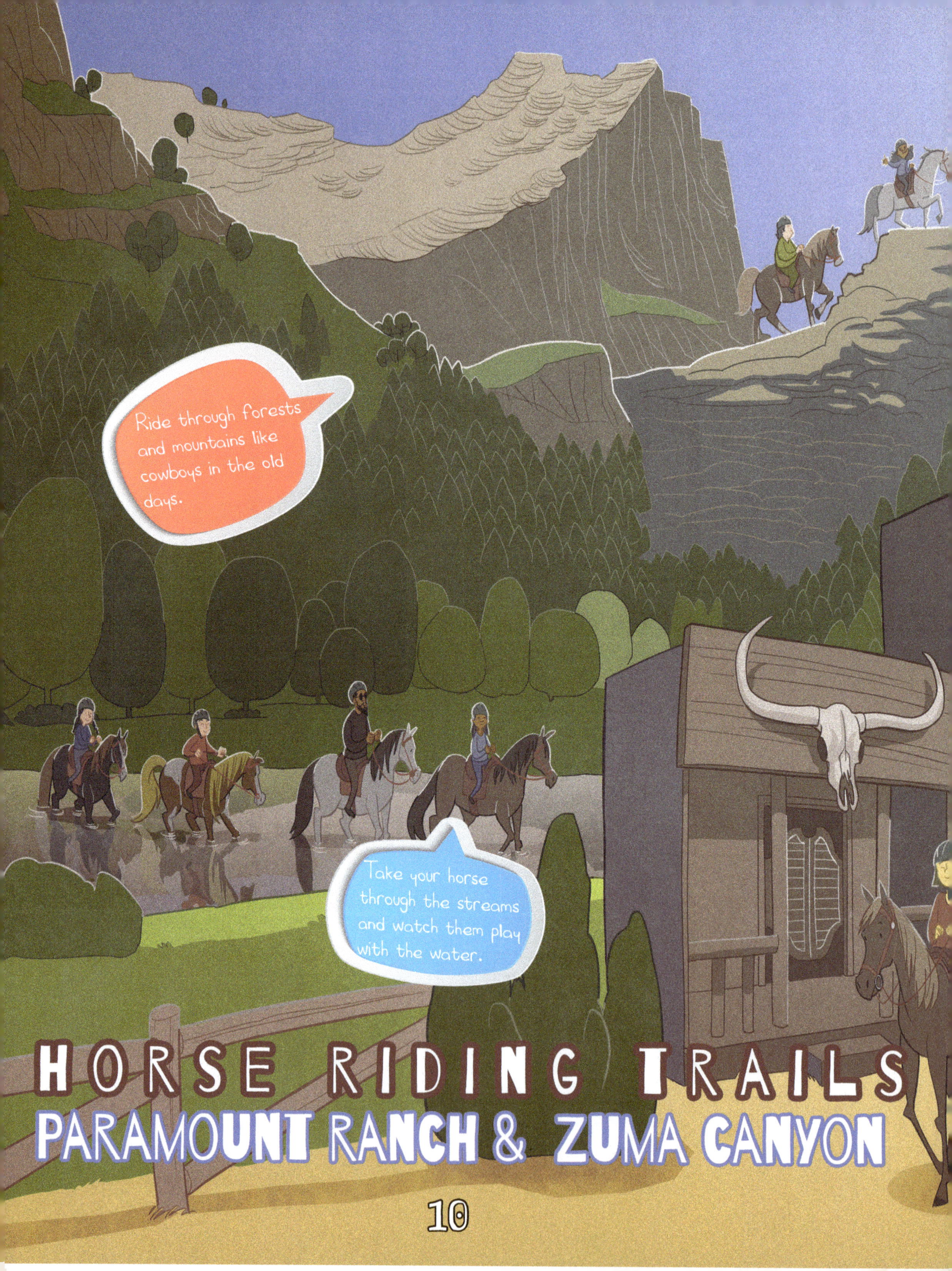

HORSE RIDING TRAILS

PARAMOUNT RANCH & ZUMA CANYON

View the Pacific Ocean from the top of a mountain.

You're a cowgirl riding through a western town.

The Paramount Ranch and Zuma Canyon located in Augora Hills and Malibu are two of the most magnificent riding trails. The rides are full of forests, streams, and ocean views. Lots of western movies and television shows have been filmed here. Some of the sets still remain, making it look like an actual western town. Yee haw!

Interesting Fact: In 1956, the Paramount Ranch created a famous auto speedway called Paramount Ranch Racetrack. But the track soon got a reputation as being too dangerous and had to close in 1957.

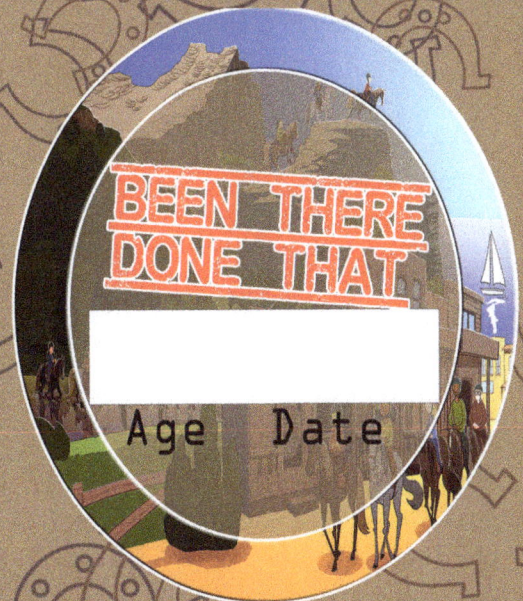

BEEN THERE DONE THAT

Age   Date

Sing and dance at the FREE summer concerts.

THE GETTY CENTER

Have a picnic near the beautiful garden.

12

The Getty Center, located in Los Angeles, opened in 1997. It is a museum known for its art, architecture, gardens, and views overlooking Los Angeles. In the summer, the Getty holds a free outdoor music series for kids and their families in the Central Garden. It features some of the most famous children's musical artists from around the world.

While visiting, please make sure to stop by the family room created just for kids. Lots and lots of cool stuff is in there.

Fun Fact: The Getty hires a herd of goats each spring to eat up brush on the mountain side of the building. This helps to reduce the risk of a mountain fire.

Draw your very own pictures of sculptures just like all of the fancy artists.

Roll down the hill on the grass. It's a tradition!

BEEN THERE DONE THAT

Age   Date

Be amazed by all of the spiffy Christmas decorations.

Visit with Santa outside on the corner.

Beverly Hills is a city located next to Los Angeles and Hollywood that was started in 1914. It is known for being home to movie stars, singers and expensive stores.

Christmas is one of the best times to visit because the city is decorated with some of the fanciest ornaments and structures. Also, Santa and Mrs. Claus take over the corner of Rodeo Drive and Wilshire Boulevard. Santa visits with all of the children while Mrs. Claus gives tours of Beverly Hills on a trolley. This makes Beverly Hills a magical place during the Christmas holiday season.

Interesting fact: Why do people pronounce Rodeo Drive...roh-day-oh instead of roh-dee-oh?
Rodeo is originally a Spanish word, so citizens pronounce it as it sounds in Spanish... Roh-Day-Oh.

BEEN THERE DONE THAT

Age   Date

LA BREA TAR PITS & LACMA

16

Watch the Metropolis II sculpture in action. The imaginary city is filled with over 1,000 running miniature vehicles as well as a train.

Play tag running through Jesus Rafael Soto's Penetrable.

The La Brea Tar Pits are a group of actual tar pits that were discovered centuries ago in what is now Hancock Park in Los Angeles. Long ago, thousands of animals would get stuck in the tar and die. The tar actually helped to preserve the animals. Over the years, researchers have dug up most of these animals, resulting in over 3 million magnificent looking fossils! Most of these fossils are now on display in the museum.

The Los Angeles County Museum of Art (LACMA), formed in 1961, has more than 150,000 works of art, including the amazing Chris Burden's Urban Light exhibit, which is 202 lamp posts from the 1920s and 1930s lined up together.

Interesting fact: Most of the animals found in the tar pits are predators. Researchers have a couple of ideas, but haven't figured out the mystery.

BEEN THERE DONE THAT

Age   Date

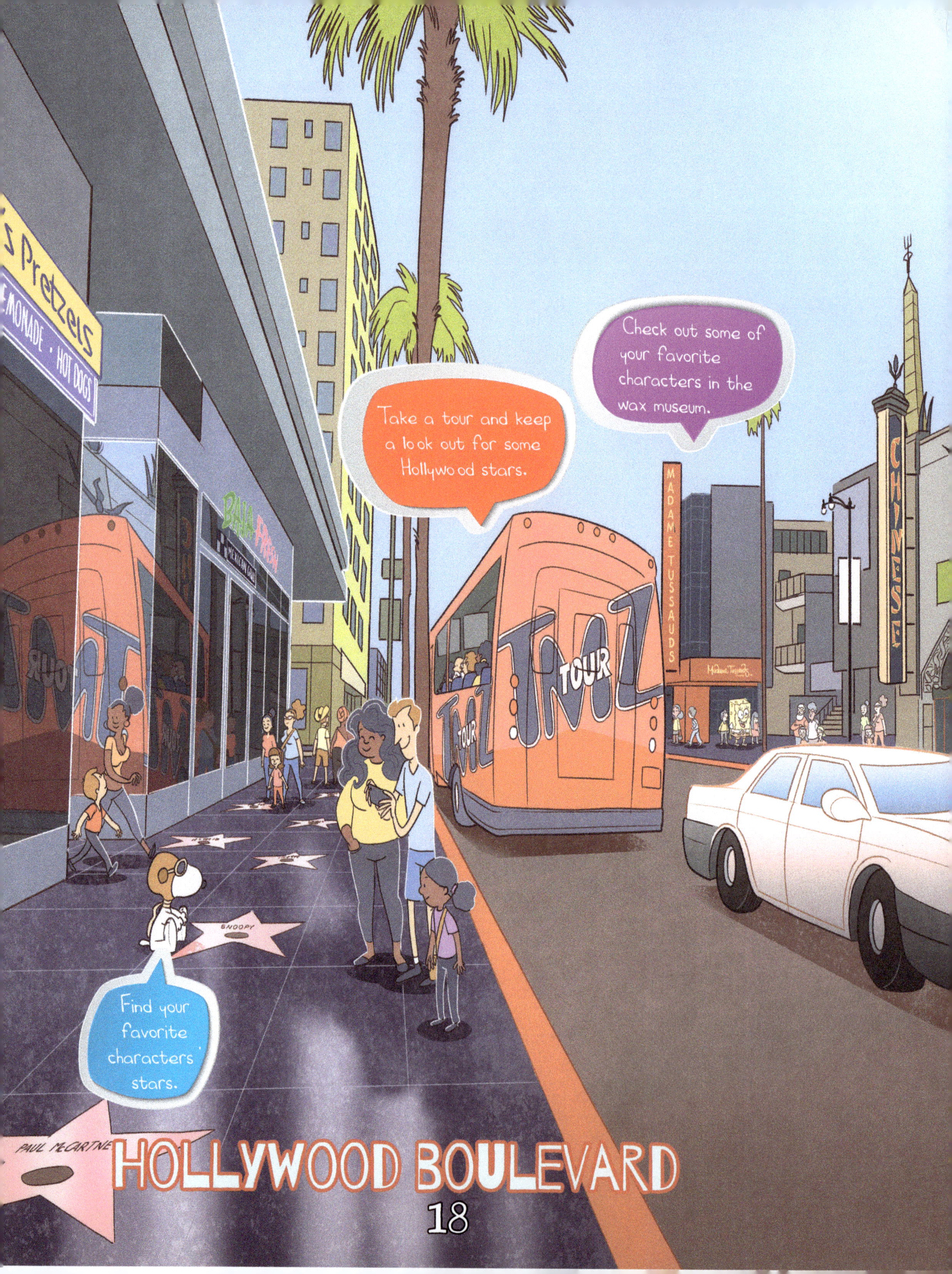

HOLLYWOOD BOULEVARD

Hollywood Boulevard, located in Hollywood, is one of the most famous streets in the world. In 1958, eight stars were laid down on the sidewalk to create the current Hollywood Walk of Fame. Now there are over 2,500 stars along 15 blocks. Most of the stars feature movie stars, singers, and directors, but also include cartoon and puppet characters like Snoopy, Kermit, Shrek and many others. The street is often packed with live costumed characters. It is one zany boulevard.

Interesting fact: Did you know a person can have more than one star? Yep, Gene Autry, The Singing Cowboy, has 5 stars. An entertainer can get a star for any of these five categories: radio, recording, motion pictures, television, and live theater. Autry is the only person to get a star for every category. Wow!

Take pictures with street performers posing as your favorite characters.

BEEN THERE DONE THAT

Age   Date

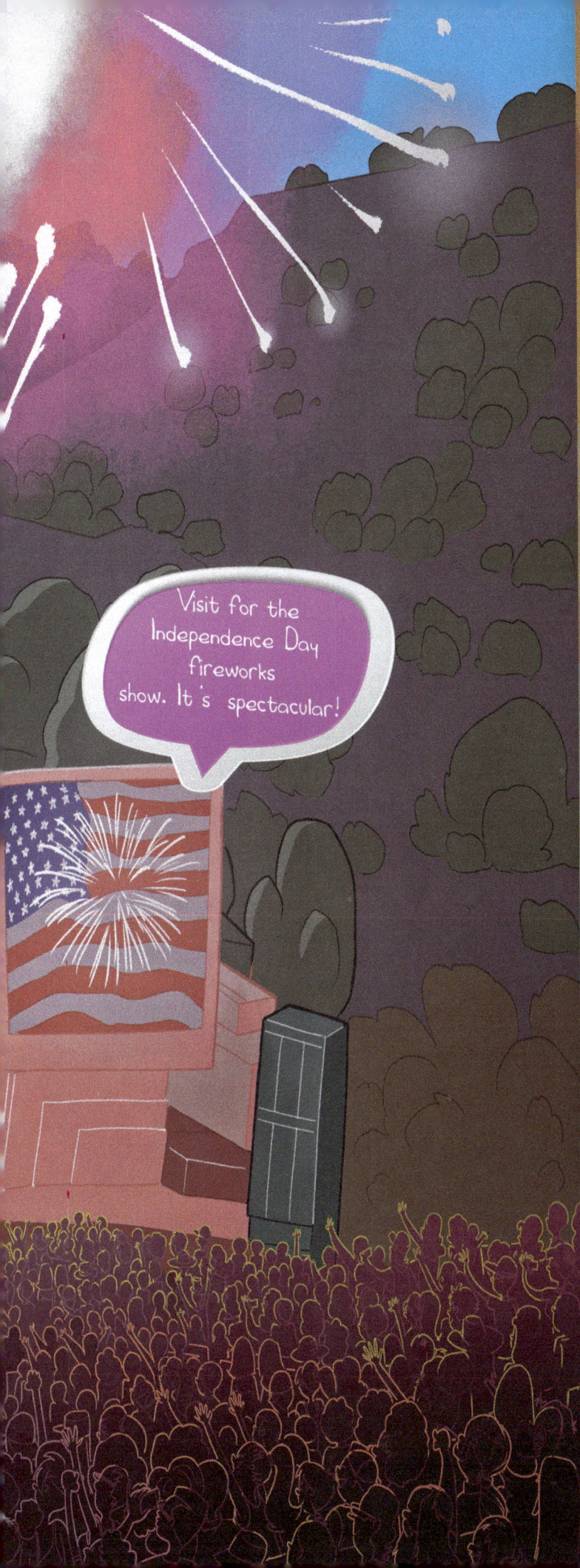

Visit for the Independence Day fireworks show. It's spectacular!

The Hollywood Bowl opened in 1922 and is the largest outdoor amphitheater in the world. It's called a bowl because of the way the hills look next to it. Famous musicians from all over the world come here to perform.

Every summer, there is a SummerSounds Children's Festival allowing kids a chance to explore different cultures of music through arts, crafts and interactive concert experiences.

Fun fact: Raccoons, squirrels, deer, lizards, and fox who live in the woods surrounding the Hollywood Bowl also love the music. Once, a fox casually came onstage and sat down next to one of the performers for 20 minutes. Maybe the fox was waiting to do the foxtrot?

BEEN THERE DONE THAT

Age   Date

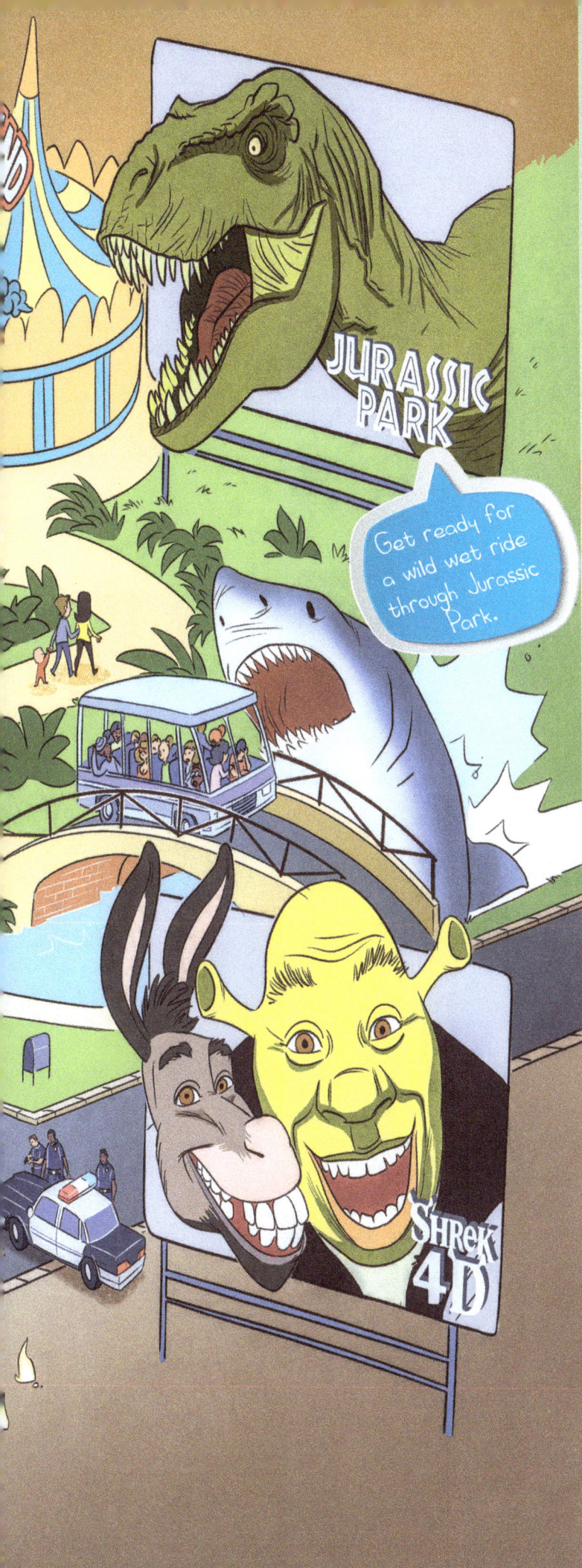

Get ready for a wild wet ride through Jurassic Park.

JURASSIC PARK

SHREK 4D

Universal Studios is a film studio and theme park located in Universal City. The studio was formed in 1912 and then opened to the public in 1915. Initially, visitors came to only picnic and watch the production of Universal's latest movie. Eventually, more attractions were added and it became a theme park just like Disneyland.

Universal Studios is also known for creating one of the most creative Halloween experiences. The park is transformed into Halloween Horror Nights with terror trams and mazes. YIKES!

Fun fact: Universal stopped allowing visitors for about 30 years beginning in the 1930's. Why? Films had changed from silent to sound so now visitors and tour buses were too loud during filming. Eventually, in 1964, they figured out a solution and reopened to the public.

BEEN THERE DONE THAT

Age   Date

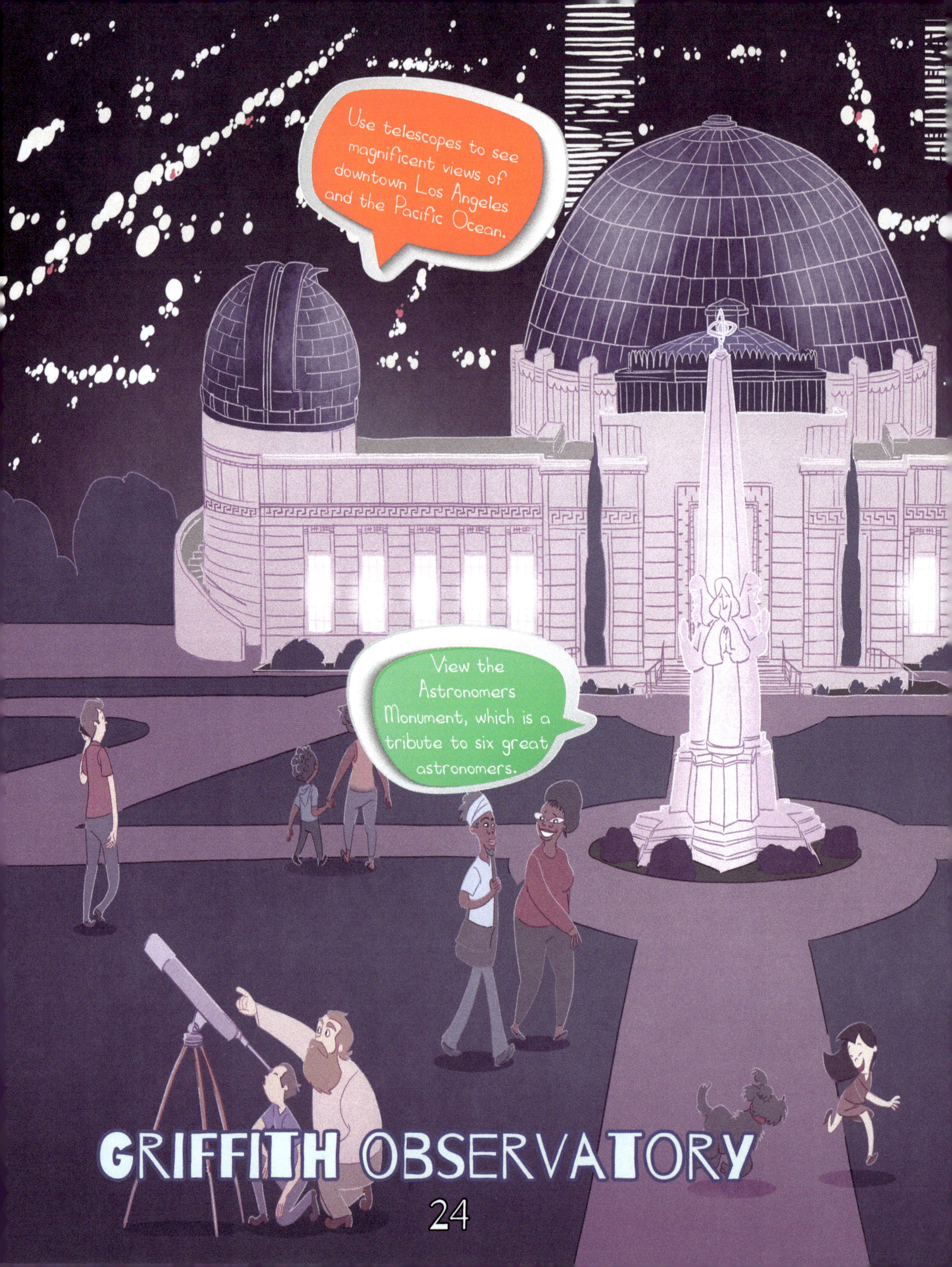

GRIFFITH OBSERVATORY

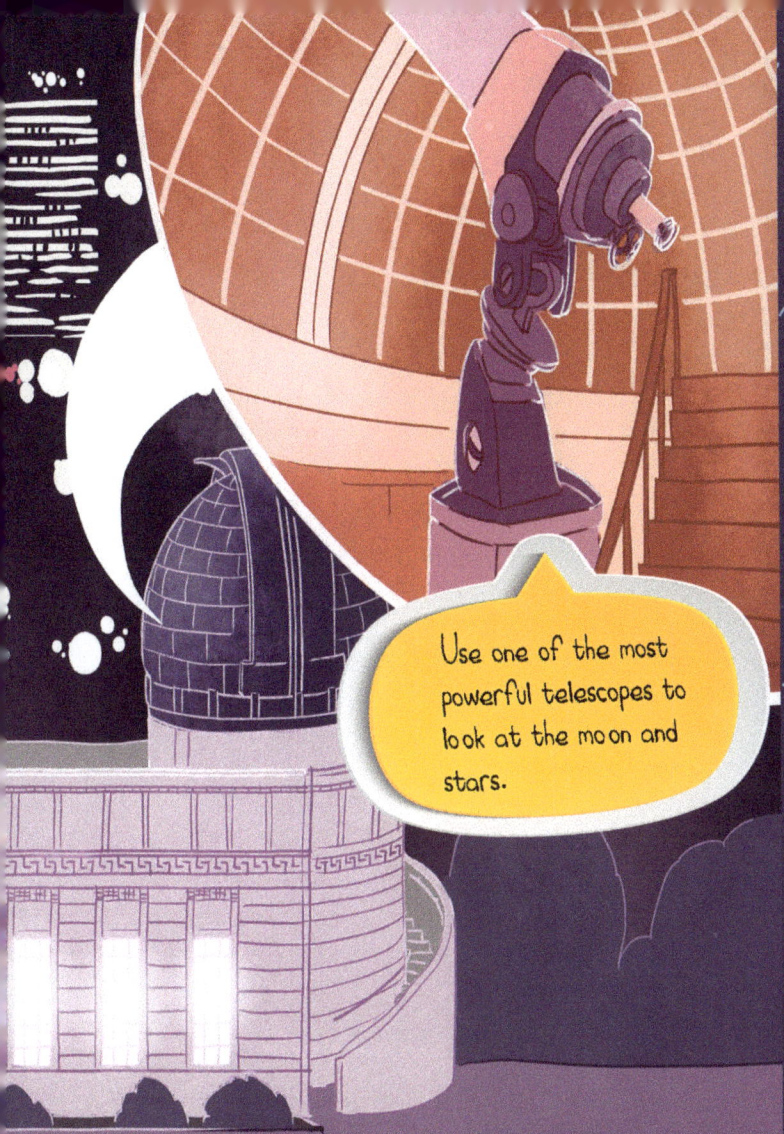

Use one of the most powerful telescopes to look at the moon and stars.

Griffith Observatory opened in 1935 and is named after Colonel Griffith J. Griffith (His first name is the same as his last name!). He wanted to create a place where anybody could just walk in and use a powerful telescope to view the moon, planets and any other shiny objects in the galaxy for free admission.

The observatory holds many educational activities and live shows in the planetarium. There are lots of exhibits including numerous forms of meteorites. If you want to learn more about space, this is the place to visit.

Interesting fact: Albert Einstein was originally to be included in the Astronomers Monument, but it didn't seem right because he was still living. Back in those days, statues were usually reserved for the non-living.

Bring your own telescope and learn all about space.

BEEN THERE DONE THAT

Age   Date

ROSE PARADE

26

The Rose Parade, located in Pasadena, is a part of America's celebration of the new year. Starting in 1890, it was originally held to gloat to the rest of the world about the weather and beauty of SoCal during mid winter. Eventually, the parade grew into a world event complete with impressive floats, remarkable bands, and majestic horses. Floats only have to follow one rule: they must be made up of only flowers.

Interesting fact: Dead flowers can also be used to decorate floats.

Get a good seat up close and cheer on the parade.

Sing and listen to bands from all over the world.

ROSE PARADE

BEEN THERE DONE THAT

Age   Date

After Friday games in the summer, you can run on the field and watch fireworks.

THINK BLUE

Dodgers

After Sunday games, kids can run the bases!

DODGERS STADIUM

Dodger stadium opened in 1962 and is the third oldest ballpark in Major League Baseball. It is home to the Los Angeles Dodgers. It is one of the most beautiful sports settings in the world because it sits on a hill with views of downtown Los Angeles on one side and the San Gabriel Mountains on the other side.

It is also home of the famous Dodger dog, which was created in 1962.

Interesting fact: The Dodger dog was originally sold with the title of a foot long hot dog, but fans complained that it was only ten inches. So, the creator, Thomas Arthur, changed the name from footlong to Dodger dog.

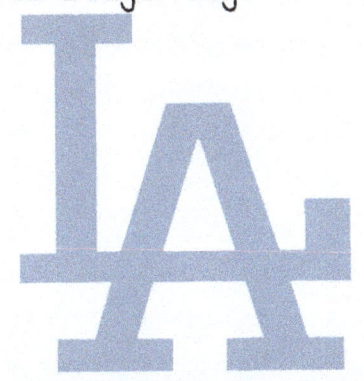

STAPLES CENTER

SHAQUILLE O'NEAL

Look for all of the championship banners.

JERRY WEST

WAYNE GRETZKY

CHICK HEARN

See statues of Los Angeles' most famous sports figures.

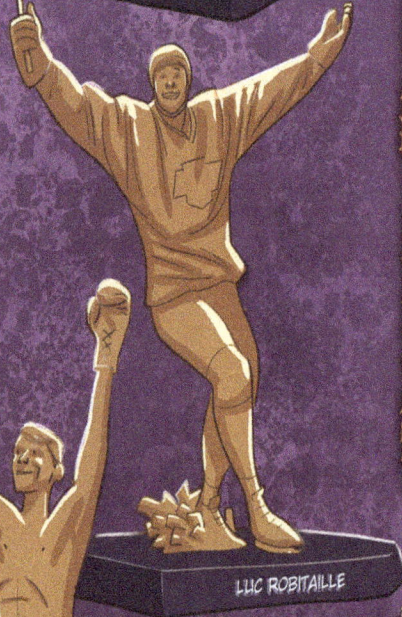

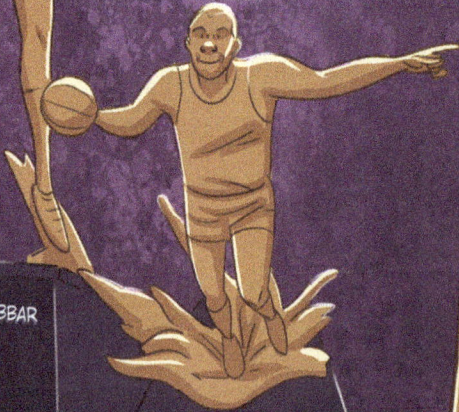

LUC ROBITAILLE

OSCAR

KAREEM ABDUL JABBAR

MAGIC JOHNSON

OSCAR DE LA HOYA

STAPLES CENTER

30

NBA.COM

Check out a hockey game with the Kings.

Watch a basketball game with the Lakers, Clippers, or Sparks.

Staples Center opened in 1999 and is a multipurpose sports arena located in Los Angeles. It is home to three basketball teams: Los Angeles Lakers, Los Angeles Clippers, and Los Angeles Sparks. It is also home to the hockey team, Los Angeles Kings. Outside the arena is Star Plaza, which features bronze statues of Los Angeles' most successful sports figures.

Staples Center is also used for music concerts, boxing matches, X Games, and even the Grammy Music Awards. Coincidentally, the Grammy Museum is right next door to the Staples Center. You should check it out too.

Interesting fact: The Clippers are the only team to not have a championship banner hanging in the Staples Center. The Lakers, Kings, and Sparks all have championship banners.

BEEN THERE DONE THAT

Age   Date

Venice Beach, located in Los Angeles, is a famous beach in SoCal. It is known for its circus boardwalk, which has street performers, skateboard and weightlifting competitions, artists and unusual characters. It is also known as Muscle Beach because there is an outdoor gym right on the beach.

Venice Beach is one of the greatest places to people watch. It is actually the second most visited tourist site in SoCal behind Disneyland.

Fun fact: The V sculpture seen on the shore does not stand for Venice. It's actually two steel arms reaching for the sky, called "Declaration". The sculpture was only supposed to be there for six months, but it fit in so well, it stayed.

Age   Date

Ride the Ferris Wheel right over the Pacific Ocean.
Play over 200 video games in the Playland Arcade.
SANTA MONICA BEACH

Santa Monica Beach, located in Santa Monica, is one of the most famous beaches in the world. The Santa Monica Pier is the most popular spot on the beach. It features an amusement park, fishing, carnival games, video games, restaurants, and of course, awesome views of the Pacific Ocean.

Located right below the pier is the Santa Monica Pier Aquarium. Check out the cool ocean life there.

Interesting fact: Santa Monica Beach was the original Muscle Beach. Weightlifters and other athletes worked out near the shore. They drew big crowds, which eventually upset vendors on the pier. The vendors complained that the athletes were stopping visitors from spending money on the pier. So the city removed all of the workout equipment and the athletes moved to Venice Beach.

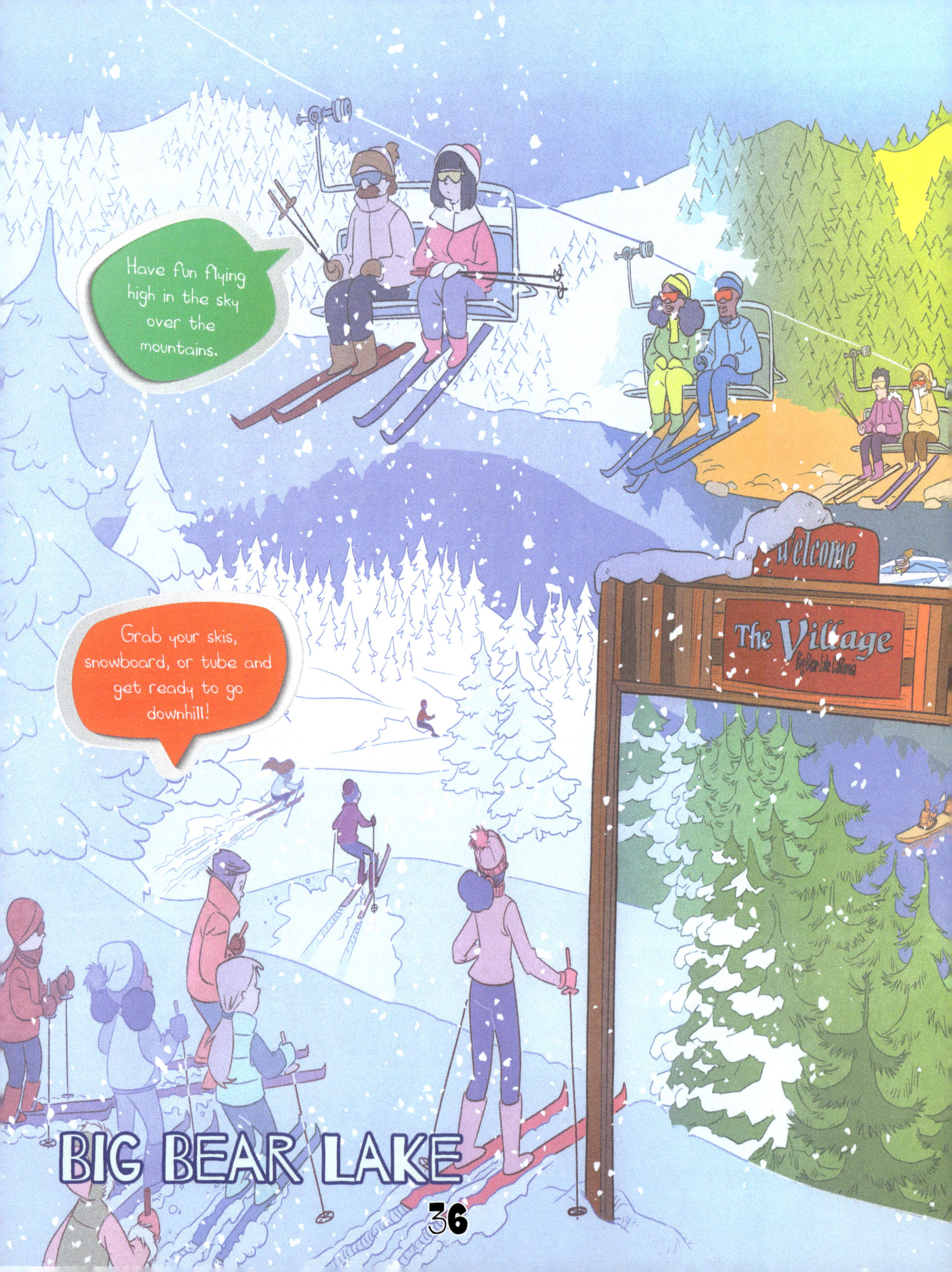

BIG BEAR LAKE

Big Bear Lake is a city right outside Los Angeles. Long ago, Big Bear Lake was only known by the local Indians and grizzly bears. But once gold was discovered, the area became flooded with people. Now that there were so many people in the area, they needed some fun things to do, so two ski resorts were built. Now it is one of the most popular summer and winter recreational places in SoCal.

So, are you surprised that you can ski in SoCal? Yep, SoCal has it all. If you're lucky, you can go to the beach and the slopes on the same day.

Interesting fact: Big Bear Lake is actually a man made lake. It's still pretty and lots of fun!

Grab your bike for a ride in the mountains.

Ride a kayak or banana boat in the lake.

Louie Welcomes you to Big Bear Lake California

BEEN THERE DONE THAT

Age   Date

CAMPING

SKIING

Take a ride on the Calico Mine filled with characters and special light effects.

Eat at Mrs. Knott's Chicken Dinner Restaurant for some fried chicken, buttermilk biscuits, and boysenberry pie.

KNOTT'S BERRY FARM

Knott's Berry Farm, located in Buena Park, actually sits on a berry farm, which was owned by Walter Knott and his family. The Knotts sold berries, berry preserves, and pies along a busy roadside. Eventually, the Knotts also started selling fried chicken on the property in a restaurant called Mrs. Knott's Chicken Dinner Restaurant. The restaurant became such a popular tourist spot that the Knotts began to build other shops and attractions that eventually turned this berry farm into a full fledged amusement park.

During the Halloween season, the park turns into Knott's Scary Farm. Prepare to be frightened!

Fun Fact: Walt Disney and Walter Knott were casual friends. They often visited each other's parks and shared information to improve them.

Scream all the way to the top of Xcelerator!

Enjoy a world dedicated to Peanuts characters at Camp Snoopy.

BEEN THERE DONE THAT

Age   Date

Toon Town created just for younger kids.

Board a real submarine and go underwater on the Finding Nemo Submarine Voyage.

TOMORROWLAND

Ride a space coaster in Space Mountain.

Located in Anaheim is Walt Disney's dream of the happiest place on earth. Walt Disney dreamed of a place full of imagination that would be fun for both children and adults. The park opened in 1955 and has been the most visited amusement park in the world.

The parade of Disney characters and the fireworks show is a must see while visiting Disneyland.

In 2015, Disney announced that it is creating a Star Wars Land, which promises to be amazing. The picture of this area in this book is a guess of what it might look like based on concept pictures.

Fun Fact: Mickey and Minnie Mouse each have over 200 outfits. Those are a lot of outfits for a mouse.

STAR WARS

BEEN THERE DONE THAT

Age   Date

Race around in cars just like in the Cars movie at Radiator Springs.
Shoot targets as you ride through a 4D experience at Toy Story Midway Mania.
Square dance in tractors at Mater's Junkyard Jamboree.
DISNEY CALIFORNIA ADVENTURE

Located across the street from the happiest place on earth is another amusement park, Disney California Adventure Park. It opened in 2001. It used to be the parking lot for Disneyland until it was converted to a theme park dedicated to the history and culture of California.

In 2012, the park created a Cars land inspired by the Disney-Pixar movie, Cars. The main attraction has been the Radiator Springs Racers, which begins with following the story of the Cars movie, and ends with a wild race with others cars on the track. It's a fun and speedy adventure!

Interesting Fact: The Pacific Wharf bridge simulates a California earthquake every so often, as it will subtly vibrate.

Watch a magnificent water show, World of Color-Season of Light, at night.

BEEN THERE DONE THAT

Age   Date

Balboa Island Pier, located in Newport Beach, is another famous tourist spot for water fun in SoCal. It features beaches, arcades, aquariums, boat rides, and other fun activities.

Balboa Fun Zone has a carnival feel to it, with a Ferris wheel, arcade, and plenty of candy! After leaving the Fun Zone, you can take a boat ride to look for whales and dolphins out in the beautiful Pacific Ocean.

You should also visit during the Christmas season when the annual Newport Beach Boat Parade & Ring of Lights is held. As many as 150 boats filled with Christmas decorations parade through the harbor. It is a spectacular sight to see.

Fun Fact: Frozen banana on a stick and dipped in chocolate was invented here. Make sure to get one when you visit!

Fly in the sky over the ocean on a parasail.

BEEN THERE DONE THAT

Age   Date

CATALINA ISLAND

Grab a kayak and float out in the ocean for some cool water fun.

Pretend you're a pirate exploring a new island.

Grab your gear to go snorkeling and scuba diving!

Santa Catalina Island, or just Catalina Island as it is commonly called, is an island just off the coast of SoCal. A long time ago, the island was mainly used for smuggling, otter hunting, and gold digging.

In the 1920's, William Wrigley Jr. bought the island and added many attractions and buildings to help make it a fun place for people to visit. It is the perfect place for water, land and even air activities. Have fun ziplining, biking, hiking, kayaking, snorkeling and so much other cool stuff.

Interesting Fact: How did the buffaloes get to the island? 14 buffaloes were flown to the island to be part of a movie. The buffaloes didn't make it into the movie and also got left behind. Today, there are about 150 buffaloes

BEEN THERE DONE THAT

Age   Date

Go to driving school and get your Legoland driver's license.

Check out some amazing Lego structures in Miniland USA.

Visit "Build and Test" to make your own Lego car and race it against others.

LEGOLAND CALIFORNIA

Located in Carlsbad is a theme park and aquarium based on the the popular building blocks, Legos. In 1999, it was the first Lego park to open in the United States. The park features massive Lego structures of famous places in the United States, like the Golden Gate Bridge, the Capitol Building in Washington, D.C., Mardi Gras in New Orleans, and the Las Vegas Strip. If you love building things, then Legoland is a place you have to go.

Fun fact: Are those massive Lego structures put together by hand? Yes, but usually a computer program is used to figure out how many Legos are needed. Then a group of workers complete the structures by hand. A special kind of glue is also used so that it will hold up to the weather. Oh yeah, all of the Legos are standard size. None of them are cut to fit.

Ride the water waves on ski jets at Aquazone Wave Racers!

BEEN THERE DONE THAT

Age   Date

SoCal has some of the biggest county fairs in America. The fairs include Ventura County Fair, Los Angeles County Fair, Orange County Fair, and San Diego County Fair. SoCal Fairs are a little bit different than amusement parks. These fairs usually have many unusual kinds of foods, such as a donut burger. Also, you will see lots of cool stuff with animals, like the largest alligator in the world and pig, duck, and goose races.

There are also many concerts and live shows at fairs. There is a little bit of everything to do and see at one of the county fairs.

Interesting fact: What's the difference between a carnival, circus, and fair? A carnival usually has several rides, games, food and few events. A circus is usually held in one big tent featuring people and animals with unusual skills. A fair has a large presence of farm animals, rides, games, and special events.

BEEN THERE DONE THAT

Age   Date

CORN

Look out for the peacock walking around showing its feathers.

The Skyfari aerial tram gives you a fantastic view from the sky.

Hop on the open air tour bus to learn more about the animals.

SAN DIEGO ZOO

Watch the polar bears swim around in their pool.

You get to feed the giraffes!

The San Diego Zoo, which opened in 1916, is one of the largest zoos in the world. It has over 3,700 animals with over 650 different species. The zoo is known for its giant panda bears. The Giant Panda Discovery Center has really great exhibits that let you experience all kinds of things, such as the pandas' smell and sounds.

The zoo also has one of the most beautiful gardens and plant collections in the world.

Interesting fact: There's a dog paired with a cheetah in the zoo. Why? Dogs are usually great with people, but cheetahs are more cautious. Dogs share their instincts with the cheetahs so they can become more comfortable with people. It's a great friendship.

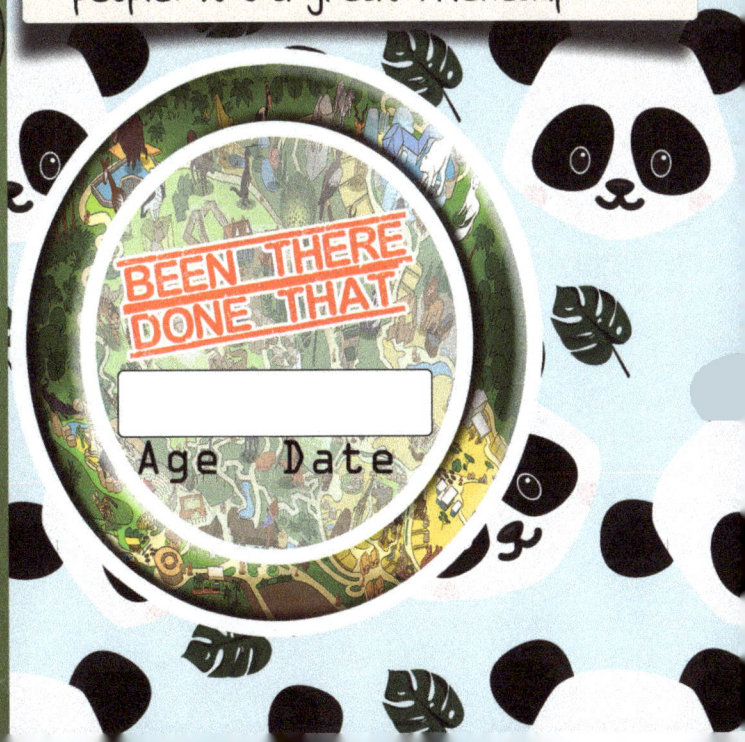

BEEN THERE DONE THAT

Age   Date

Slide down the Flightline Safari zipline for a fun look at the wildlife below.

Feed a lorikeet as it sits on your arm.

SAN DIEGO ZOO SAFARI PARK

54

The San Diego Zoo Safari Park, located in Escondido, opened in 1972. It has more than 2,600 animals with over 300 species. One of the best things about the park is that there are free areas for animals to roam. Some of the kind of animals that you will see in these areas are giraffes, rhinoceros, gazelles, cheetahs, lions and various birds.

There are also many shows to enjoy, such as watching a cheetah running at top speed or remarkable birds showing their amazing flying talents.

Fun Fact: Kids get in for free during the month of October. F-R-E-E-!-!

Get in a hot air balloon and enjoy an unbelievable view of the whole safari.

Take the open air caravan and ride close to animals roaming freely in an open area.

Watch cheetahs run at Shiley's Cheetah Run.

BEEN THERE DONE THAT

Age   Date

Take the Bayside Skyride to fly over Mission Bay.

You will laugh so hard watching the sea lions.

Check out the orcas as they swim around in their new naturalistic setting.

SEAWORLD SAN DIEGO

SeaWorld San Diego is a marine mammal theme park, that opened in 1964. It is most known for its killer whales performing amazing acrobatics. The orcas, which is another name for killer whales, no longer perform these types of shows, but you can still view these remarkable mammals in a more natural habitat.

Even though the orcas don't perform anymore, there are other mammals performing amazing feats and comedy in Sea Lions LIVE and Dolphins Days. In addition to all of the live mammal shows, there are almost 50 cool rides to explore here.

Fun Fact: Four college students dreamed up the idea of SeaWorld. It was only supposed to be an underwater restaurant. That idea was too difficult to work at the time so it changed to a marine animal theme park.

Watch "Pet's Rule", a funny show full of cats, birds, dogs, and a pig.

Enjoy a wild ride through the icy Arctic Circle.

BEEN THERE DONE THAT

Age   Date

So now you see why

SoCal is

So Cool!

Wishing you a safe journey,
Ryan